fresh hope through

New Perspectives

30 days of readings

CWR Waverley Abbey House, Waverley Lane, Farnham, Surrey GU9 8EP

National Distributors

AUSTRALIA
Christian Marketing Pty Ltd.,
PO Box 519, Belmont, Victoria 3216
Tel: (052) 413 288
CANADA
CMC Distribution Ltd.,
PO Box 7000, Niagara on the Lake,
Ontario LOS 1JO
Tel: 1–800–325–1297
MALAYSIA
Salvation Book Centre (M),
Sdn. Bhd, 23 Jalan SS2/64,
Sea Park, 47300 Petaling Jaya, Selangor
Tel: (3) 7766411
NEW ZEALAND
Christian Marketing NZ Ltd,
Private Bag,
Havelock North
Tel: 0508 535659 (toll free)
NIGERIA
FBFM, Medium Housing Estate, Block 34, Flat 6,
Glover St., E.M., Lagos, PO Box 70952, Victoria Island
Tel: (01) 611160/866451
REPUBLIC OF IRELAND
Scripture Union
40 Talbot Street, Dublin 1
Tel: (01) 8363764
SINGAPORE
Campus Crusade Asia Ltd.,
315, Outram Road
06–08 Tan Boon Liat Building,
Singapore 0316
Tel; (65) 2223640
SOUTH AFRICA
Struik Christian Books (Pty Ltd)
PO Box 193, Maitland 7405,
Cape Town
Tel: (021) 551 5900
USA
CMC Distribution, PO Box 644,
Lewiston, New York 14092–0644
Tel: 1–800–325–1297

Strength to Care. Copyright © 1996 by Hilary Vogel
Published 1996 by CWR
Cover design: CWR Production
Design and typesetting: CWR Production
Printed in Great Britain by Wace Corporate Print, Poole
ISBN 1 85345 103 7

Unless otherwise identified, all Scripture quotations in this publication are from the Holy Bible: New International Version (NIV). Copyright © 1973, 1978, 1984, International Bible Society.

strength to
CARE
Encouragement for Carers

Hilary Vogel

Biography

Hilary Vogel has been involved in Christian ministry with her husband, Philip, for 38 years. She helps to lead a carer's support group in their church and works part-time at a Christian-based hostel for women. This, along with seeking to support her elderly parents, has given her a greater awareness of the needs of those caring for others. She lives in Guildford, Surrey and has three children and five grandchildren.

Biography

Know

Whom You are Serving

"... whatever you did for one of the least of these brothers of mine, you did for me." Matthew 25:40.

Caring encompasses a vast field of human relationships. It may be caring for someone at home twenty-four hours a day, or struggling to help elderly relatives many miles away, involving much travelling, and times of anxiety and uncertainty. It may involve a lifetime's commitment for a handicapped child, or an elderly parent who has ceased to recognise you, or appreciate what you are doing, or a disabled partner.

Whatever the situation, our lives can be filled with the demands of others, and helping to deal with their physical and emotional needs. We may not have set out to serve them in this way, but because we love them we find ourselves in the position of a servant. Then we are in good company! The greatest servant example we have in the world is Jesus, who being in the very nature of God, made Himself nothing, and took on Himself the nature of a servant (Philippians 2).

He not only taught and encouraged His disciples to serve one another, He lived out His words by His lifestyle, when for example He took a towel, knelt before His disciples and washed their feet. He was a servant through and through, it was epitomised in everything He did, yet He was able to balance servanthood with fulfilling His destiny in God. Jesus was able to be fully in control and living the way God wanted Him to, yet always with the evidence of a servant-heart, caring and ministering to those He met. The motive for His actions was always to do the will of His heavenly Father with a heart of love.

If asked what our motives are as carers, some would

immediately say love – I am committed to this person because I love them. Others might find themselves in a position of duty – even though they love the person they find that no one else is available to care for them – so have filled a gap. Others may even feel they've been lumbered, because those who should be taking responsibility have shied away. Whatever the motive, remember God knows your heart. If your prime motive in life is your commitment to God, then this is the bedrock of your life and everything else can be constructed on the foundation of your service to God.

God knows your circumstances better than you do. Have you ever thought that God knows the stresses we are under and the difficulties that we face? He knows when problems accumulate and others don't pull their weight. He knows the burdens we carry and the desires of our hearts.

So let's focus on God, and acknowledge that He is the One we are serving. Let's be open with Him, not only about our practical needs, but also about our feelings and our weaknesses, and as we serve Him, allow Him to become master of our situation, then we can feel able to trust our loved ones into His care.

For reflection and action:

❧ *Jesus said that if you give a cup of cold water in His name then you are serving Him.*

❧ *Remember God knows your heart.*

Living for God

"Live as children of light."

Ephesians 5:8

There is no greater contrast in the world than that between darkness and light, and God has transferred us from one to the other through our salvation in Christ. Paul tells us in Ephesians 5:8–10 *"For you were once darkness, but now you are light in the Lord. Live as children of light ... and find out what pleases the Lord."*

Surely this must be one of the greatest miracles ever performed, that from a situation of spiritual blindness and no experience of God in our lives, He has brought us into the light of His love and knowledge of Him.

God has given us a new life where He reigns as King, and we, His children, have all the privileges of royalty. Through the sacrificial death of Jesus, we have not only come into a place of total freedom, but the past wrongs have been dealt with and forgotten. We are now free as God's redeemed people, to live lives which are transparent and pleasing to Him.

It's easy to be idealistic about living in spiritual harmony with God until we are suddenly brought back down to earth by the intrusion of everyday life, with its pressures and the added responsibility that caring demands.

Far from pleasing God, there are times when I feel like one of those jugglers who spins plates on long sticks, then spends all his time running back and forth in an attempt to keep them from crashing down. And if things don't go according to plan, then a sense of failure creeps in followed with a liberal dose of self-condemnation, and soon I find myself on one of those downward spirals where, "I don't feel like praying today – and even if I did, I'm not sure if God would hear me." The defeatist attitude has set in, and the best I can hope for is that things will improve tomorrow. Have you ever felt like that?

So let's be realistic about this, how can we live as children of light – pleasing the Lord? The only answer that I know is, moment by moment and step by step in partnership with God. Here are some steps to consider:

Keep the channels of communication open and be willing to hear God. Start where you are. If you don't feel like praying, say, "Lord I don't feel like praying, but I want You to help me to change, I want to live a life pleasing to You." Tell God all that's going on inside you. Ask Him to do a miracle in your life. Ask Him to lift you up and encourage you. Have some expectation of what you want God to do for you. Remember that you and God are in this together.

Read God's Word and ask Him to speak to you, personally, through the pages.

Allow yourself to be inspired by Jesus the Light of the World. Jesus said *"I am the light of the world. Whoever follows me will never walk in darkness, but will have the light of life"* (John 8:12).

For reflection and action:

❧ *If you don't expect God to work in your life today, then you probably won't be disappointed.*

❧ *Find a friend for mutual prayer, support and encouragement.*

Don't
Give
Up

"... that you may be mature and complete." James 1:4

Facing trials is never joyous, but overcoming them can have exciting rewards, with lasting benefits from the lessons learned.

In James 1:2–4 we read, *"Consider it pure joy, my brothers, whenever you face trials of many kinds, because you know that the testing of your faith develops perseverance. Perseverance must finish its work so that you may be mature and complete, not lacking anything."*

For most of us life is like an assault course with many obstacles, the degree of difficulty varying with each person's set of circumstances. If you've seen people tackling an assault course, you only have to look at their faces to know that there is very little joy found in grappling with the demands imposed on them. But at the end their faces have taken on a different expression. Even through fatigue and near exhaustion, there is a sense of achievement from having conquered the course. There is a sense of fulfilment to be found as each apparently insurmountable problem is dealt with, and lessons are learned.

The assault course of our daily life can be equally as daunting; just waking up in the morning with the prospect of facing a new day with all its responsibilities and decision-making could find us hiding under the sheets for fear of what lies ahead.

The apostle Paul said that we don't need to fear or hide, but to see each new day as a challenge, because we are going to learn so much through the trials that we face, and that the Christian life is one of perseverance. It is God's desire that we should become *"mature and complete, not lacking anything"*. We need to be able to trust Him through each moment of the day, and we will learn as we go along.

God's ways are always based on a simple childlike approach, and perseverance is something we can often learn from a child.

I remember the frustration I experienced when my children went through the phase of learning to tie their own shoe laces, and didn't want to be helped. We'd be in a hurry to go out somewhere but the shoe laces were not tied, and it seemed as though it would take all day, as the little fingers struggled to loop the laces round each other with a concentration that eclipsed the need for us to hurry. But by going through this process of perseverance they gradually became more adept at the task until they had mastered it to perfection, and learnt a lesson for life.

If you stop for a moment, can you recall ways in which God has taken you through trials and difficulties with His enabling grace, and has taught you lessons in perseverance? If so then you will recognise that this is all part of God's plan to bring you to maturity and completeness in Him. The lessons of life go on day by day, so let us put ourselves completely in His hands, especially as we seek to serve those that we are caring for. Let us take encouragement from Hebrews 12, fixing our eyes on Jesus so that we can run with perseverance the race marked out for us.

For reflection and action:

❧ *Perseverance is never giving up.*

❧ *Learn to be more childlike in your relationship with God.*

Discipleship

"Follow me." John 1:43

Jesus speaks a number of times about the cost of following Him. In Luke 14:27 He says, *"Anyone who does not carry his cross and follow me cannot be my disciple"*, and in verse 33, *"Any of you who does not give up everything he has cannot be my disciple"*.

In simple terms, Jesus is telling us to put Him first and foremost in our lives, and let nothing come between us. He is also telling us to count the cost, to ask ourselves whether we are prepared to make all our resources available in total commitment to Him. He wants us to let go of our personal ambitions and claims to fame and fortune, in fact to surrender our rights to everything, even human relationships, in the light of our relationship with Him. He may well choose to give us some, or all, of these things in His plan and in His time, or He may not, but He wants to have that place of choice and lordship in our lives.

We may find it hard to understand what taking up our cross is all about. The idea may seem to be irksome and weighty, and as carers we perhaps feel that we already have enough to carry. Some may even feel as though they are carrying a cross, because of the difficulty of their circumstances.

The principle of Jesus taking up His cross was not the burden of it, but the willingness. He laid aside everything else, facing His only objective, that of doing His Father's will. He could say to His Father, "not my will, but yours be done".

We are told in Philippians 2:5, *"Your attitude should be the same as that of Christ Jesus"*, an attitude of meekness and humility which meant that He was freely available to God.

Discipleship is always based on an attitude of heart and mind, and the willingness and obedience which follows. Jesus never forces us into a relationship with Himself, it is entirely optional. We need to consider our position with Him, and the depth of commitment we are prepared to make. The more we know and appreciate God's redeeming work in our lives, the simpler taking up our cross can become.

Paul took up his cross from the moment of his amazing encounter with Jesus. He let go of everything both past and personal, in order that he might know God in the deepest relationship possible. His conversion was so life-changing, that knowing God became his consuming passion, it outweighed every other desire in his life, he considered *"everything a loss compared to the surpassing greatness of knowing Christ Jesus my Lord"* (Philippians 3:8). He counted the cost and decided to stake everything on being a true disciple.

For reflection and action:

• *Let us ask ourselves how much are we prepared to count the cost of following Jesus.*

• *Taking up our cross is easier if we are not trying to hold on to other things at the same time.*

God's
Bonus

"Give, and it will be given to you." Luke 6:38

"How much more can I go on giving out?" Have you ever thought like this? Have you ever wondered how much longer your resources will last before you dry up all together? If you are a carer then your scenario is possibly that of a life given in selfless devotion to one who may not appreciate what you are doing, or worse than that, may even be hostile or antagonistic towards you in their state of incapacity. He or she is the one who you see as having the need, and you are the one with the ability to give, so you give with all you've got!

There are some carers I have known who have given of themselves in such a way that they have been denied opportunities in life which others of us would take for granted. Career prospects and the chance to climb up some of life's ladders have stayed out of reach, and the possibility of marriage and a home of their own have been shelved until too late. These are all part of the cost of giving and caring.

Paul, in his letter to the Philippians (Chapter 4:18–19), was writing to a generous-hearted people who had learnt how to give in a practical and sacrificial way. They had cared for him on his travels, they had sent gifts to make sure that he was looked after, and again here he was on the receiving end of their generosity – in his case it was practical needs being met in hospitality, money and gifts in kind. Yet Paul knew that they also had needs, and he turned round and said to them, *"My God will meet all your needs according to his glorious riches in Christ Jesus"*. This is how God works, He gives to those who give.

In Luke 6:38 Jesus says, *"Give, and it will be given to you. A good measure, pressed down, shaken together and running over, will be poured into your lap. For with the measure you use, it will be measured to you."* Our God gives generously. He sees the costly things which go unnoticed by others, like the broken nights, and the inner agonies that we suffer. He knows how drained we sometimes feel, and to those who give – He gives.

He rewards us according to His love and grace, and out of His riches, which are not only glorious, but of eternal value, which cannot be lost or destroyed. We can never outgive God.

In Romans 8:32 we read, *"He who did not spare his own Son, but gave him up for us all – how will he not also, along with him, graciously give us all things?"*

For reflection and action:

❧ *Allow yourself to receive something from God today.*

❧ *See if there are ways in which you can receive help from others.*

God's
Love

"Greater love has no-one than this, that he lay down his life for his friends." John 15:13

It is hard for us as human beings to comprehend the love of God, and to realise that we are loved by, and precious to Him. Jesus says, *"As the Father has loved me, so have I loved you"* (John 15:9). And John tells us, *"We love because he first loved us"* (1 John 4:19). God is the author and motivator of love.

We may wonder what God's love is like. We have so many ideas of love, but the very best we can understand is linked with our own experience, and our personal pilgrimage thus far.

It was from His heart of love that God took the initiative and reached out to mankind. Knowing how sinful and rebellious we had become, He chose to make the ultimate sacrifice, paying the price for our freedom, so that each of us can be blameless in His sight. This is love in the extreme, *"For a good man someone might possibly dare to die. But God demonstrates his own love for us in this: While we were still sinners, Christ died for us"* (Romans 5:7–8). I sometimes wonder if I'm really worth loving all that much.

Being a carer can at times seem to be a very mundane way of life, as we wait on others who have more needs than we do. We can feel as though we are struggling alone, somewhat adrift from society in general – almost finding ourselves in a subservient role in comparison to those out in the world who appear to be achieving great feats.

We may be very busy, and our lives taken up with tremendous amounts of planning, organising and physical work; this we give ourselves willingly to because we have a servant heart, but let us not in anyway confuse servanthood with being of less value. Jesus came to earth and chose the way of servanthood (Philippians 2:6–7). He lived His life as an example for us to follow, and was the greatest servant of all time. It makes no difference to Him whether we are high up in the church, or low down in the pew, or even if we find it hard to get to a place of worship, we are of equal value to Him, set apart, precious and dearly loved.

"This is how God showed his love among us: He sent his one and only Son into the world that we might live through him. This is love: not that we loved God, but that he loved us" (1 John 4:9–10).

For reflection and action:

۞ *Meditate on John 3:16. Does the world include you?*

۞ *Ask God to help you to receive more of His love for you.*

The
Secret
Place

"He who dwells in the shelter of the Most High will rest in the shadow of the Almighty."

Psalm 91:1

We all look for that place of rest and meeting with God, but for many of us it is all too illusive. With busy demanding lives, our main enemy is time. If you are a carer, time will be at even more of a premium. We can't "make time" or "find time", we need to allocate time.

I remember having difficulty with this during one particular phase when my children were small. Life was very busy and I was much too tired by the evening, when the children were in bed, to have a meaningful time with God. So in the mornings, when I went into the bathroom, I would take an extra five or ten minutes, so that I could meet alone with God. I usually sat on the edge of the bath, or knelt on the bath mat, and that was my secret place – which I knew was just as valid in God's eyes as anywhere else on earth. I know that we can talk with God at anytime and anywhere, while driving the car, or washing the dishes, but it is still important to have a secret place, with no distractions, where we are doing nothing but communing with God.

In Psalm 91:4 we read, *"He will cover you with his feathers, and under his wings you will find refuge."* Like the chick can know the warmth, comfort and safety of being in that intimate place with its mother, so we can know the love and protection of God in a relationship which supersedes all earthly relationships. He is wanting to be our shelter and hiding place, and we can choose to dwell with Him. I wrote the following words as a result of reflecting on this need in my own life:

How can I find that secret place, to be alone with God?
Where can I stand in peace and quiet,
reflecting on my Lord?
Just a few precious moments is all I ask –
a breathing-space, not much,
To see His face, to hear His voice and feel
His gentle touch.
Oh to be alone with Him amid the daily strife,
While the world rushes on at break-neck speed,
forgetting the meaning of life.
The world sweeps me on, making demands,
insisting I go its way,
I must go here, I must do this, there's not
enough hours in a day.
I must run the home, and run the car,
and get to work on the dot,
I must pay the mortgage, do the chores,
and have my leisure time slot.
I've time to eat, and time to sleep,
and time to watch T.V.,
So it's a false assumption for me to think
that time is my enemy.
So how can I do it, and where can I start
with the pressures all around?
I could do it now – I could "take off my shoes and stand
on holy ground."

For reflection and action:

❧ *Try it now – "take off your shoes and stand on holy ground".*

❧ *Don't just put God first in your life – but first in your timetable.*

The Better Part

"Mary has chosen what is better." Luke 10:42

Can you imagine the scene, Martha running a well organised home, then just when she thought everything was under control, some unexpected guests arrived. Let us pick up the story in Luke 10:38–42.

"As Jesus and his disciples were on their way, he came to a village where a woman named Martha opened her home to him. She had a sister called Mary, who sat at the Lord's feet listening to what he said. But Martha was distracted by all the preparations that had to be made. She came to him and asked, 'Lord, don't you care that my sister has left me to do the work by myself? Tell her to help me!'

'Martha, Martha,' the Lord answered, 'you are worried and upset about many things, but only one thing is needed. Mary has chosen what is better, and it will not be taken away from her" (Luke 10:38–42).

It seems from the text as though Jesus had just dropped in – now plans had to be made and a meal prepared, and I'm sure Martha wanted the best for Jesus. We know that she had opened her home to Him and His friends, which suggests that she was kind and welcoming, but do we detect a note of self-pity? She seems to be hoping that Jesus will take pity on her.

Self-pity is one of the most destructive elements that we can allow into our lives, it creeps in, in small ways, almost unnoticed – or in ways we feel to be justifiable, then it lodges there, and starts to fester and soon it will affect everything we do and say. Martha was in great danger of letting this happen to her, but Jesus was there with His insight and wisdom, to nip the problem in the bud. Jesus always sees the whole person and the total situation, not just the facts we present to Him, and He also knows the motives of our hearts.

If we stop for a moment and realise that this was the Mary who anointed Jesus at Bethany, pouring out the expensive anointing oil on Him, and remember the words of Jesus "whoever is forgiven much, loves much," then we can understand from a different perspective. Mary had known the transforming power of Jesus in her life, and had a very real experience of sins forgiven, and freedom from guilt, things we sometimes take for granted, but which for her had such a life-changing impact that she now lived a life-style of worship.

As carers it is encouraging to know that Jesus always recognises our labours of love and hard work, especially on behalf of others. He also sees the difference between things of lasting value and those temporal, and here He's talking in a very straight manner to Martha, telling her not to get hung up with worry about everyday needs, but rather to focus on things of eternal value. Mary's focus was on her Lord, her gratitude to Him and her awareness of her standing in Christ. That, according to Jesus, should be the paramount focus of our lives, then we too will be "choosing the better part".

For reflection and action:

❧ *Does your focus need adjusting?*

❧ *Thank God for any life-changing experience He has given you.*

Constant
Care

"Let us not become weary in
doing good." Galatians 6:9

In the New Testament we read of numerous carers who were anxious to bring their loved ones to Jesus, and went to great lengths to do so. Some walked for many hours, even days; some carried them on beds; some came in anger or desperation; some in faith and trust; but all of them were just ordinary people doing everything they could for those they loved.

Statistics tell us that in Britain today there are nearly seven million people who are looking after a relative or friend, who because of illness, disability or old age, cannot manage to look after themselves.

Carers are ordinary people who simply get on with what has to be done when someone close to them needs help. They may not think of themselves as carers, but this term is used to recognise the job they are doing. They provide various means of care, often all day, every day, sometimes for many years. This can be tiring and stressful, but they keep going because it needs to be done, and many who are Christians are also motivated by the fact that they are serving God in this way.

Jesus always teaches that we should love and care for the needy, just as He always showed compassion for them. We are taught never to do things for people because they are able to reciprocate, but when we open up our lives and our homes to invite the disadvantaged who cannot repay us, God will reward us in heaven. The principles of Jesus' teaching are always simple, and always an expression of love. The writer in Acts 20:35 says we are to remember the words of Jesus, *"It is more blessed to give than to receive."* I'm sure that most of our caring is not done from the motive of what we shall receive, but nevertheless, Jesus is always generous in rewarding our service to Him. So much of what we do goes unnoticed by the world in general, but He sees that which is done in secret and He will reward us accordingly. He also sees our hidden struggles and heartaches and has promised to stand by us, and never leave us.

Let us bring our loved ones to Him, He is always available, and more ready to listen than we are to pray, so let us reach out in faith on their behalf. If we feel that our faith is small, then let us reach out in small stages, as far as our faith will reach, which in itself will help our faith to grow. But bring them, just as they are, and just as we are, and He will bless them.

For reflection and action:

❧ *Never be afraid of asking for help and support, remember you have needs as well.*

❧ *Allow others to share the burden and so share the blessing.*

Day 10

Costly
Devotion

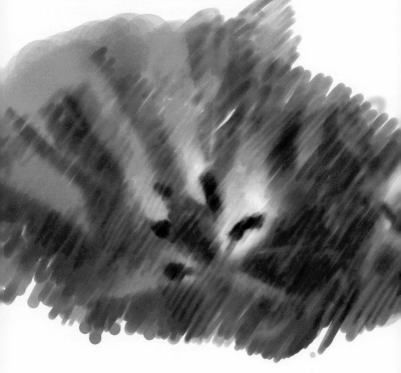

"She has done a beautiful thing to me." Mark 14:6

The story from which today's text is taken is a beautiful one, so I am going to quote it in full:

"While He [Jesus] was in Bethany, reclining at the table in the home of a man known as Simon the Leper, a woman came with an alabaster jar of very expensive perfume, made of pure nard. She broke the jar and poured the perfume on his head.

Some of those present were saying indignantly to one another, 'Why this waste of perfume? It could have been sold for more than a year's wages and the money given to the poor.' And they rebuked her harshly.

'Leave her alone,' said Jesus, 'Why are you bothering her? She has done a beautiful thing to me. The poor you will always have with you, and you can help them any time you want. But you will not always have me. She did what she could. She poured perfume on my body beforehand to prepare for my burial. I tell you the truth, wherever the gospel is preached throughout the world, what she has done will also be told, in memory of her' " (Mark 14:3–9).

I find this an amazing story, how a woman who was a social outcast and a nobody, could publicly waste probably everything she had on someone she loved. Maybe she was impetuous and impulsive, but she took what she had and used the opportunity to anoint Jesus. She demonstrated her love with everything she had. It didn't seem to matter to her that she was criticised for being extravagant or uneconomical, for sacrificial love is never economical.

There may well be times when people shake their head at the waste and extravagance of a life devoted to caring for someone who might not even be able to appreciate it. This can be a cross to bear, but a worthwhile one when put in the perspective of a loving relationship. From a heart of love we can sacrifice our time and energy for others, and lavish our love on them.

Let us read the words of 1 Corinthians 13 from the paraphrase *The Message*:

"Love never gives up.
Love cares more for others than for self.
Love doesn't want what it doesn't have.
Love doesn't strut,
Doesn't have a swelled head,
Doesn't force itself on others,
Isn't always 'me first',
Doesn't fly off the handle,
Doesn't keep score of the sins of others,
Doesn't revel when others grovel,
Takes pleasure in the flowering of truth,
Puts up with anything,
Trusts God always,
Always looks for the best,
Never looks back,
But keeps going to the end."

For reflection and action:

❧ *Mary loved much because she'd been forgiven much.*

❧ *The more we know of God's redeeming work in our lives, the more we will be able to pour out His love for others.*

Costly
Commitment

"Where you go I will go."

Ruth 1:16

When Naomi, who was a widow, decided to return from the land of Moab to her native town of Bethlehem, her daughter-in-law Ruth, who was also a widow, committed herself to standing by her and looking after her. We read her words in the first chapter of Ruth: *"Where you go I will go, and where you stay I will stay. Your people will be my people and your God my God"* (v.16).

Ruth so devoted herself to Naomi that she was prepared to go and live in a strange land in order to support her. We see Ruth as a person who was willing to put her own interests in secondary place, and step out in faith, with an uncertain future ahead, and to live a day at a time trusting God. Her love and concern for Naomi certainly took priority in her life. We also see her as a humble person, who was not only ready to take advice from the older woman, but to involve herself in the menial task of gleaning grain behind the reapers in order to support them both. I think it was also likely that she was home-sick for the family and friends that she had left behind in Moab, but her mind was set, and disregarding her own feelings, she sought to fulfil her mother-in-law's needs within the context of recognised family traditions.

Naomi knew of her late husband's relatives,

whom she thought would probably be willing to help by allowing Ruth to join the harvesters, and so that was how Ruth met Boaz.

When she first spoke to him it was as a foreigner, but straightaway he recognised her caring heart, and his words to her in Ruth 2:11–12 are, *"I've been told all about what you have done for your mother-in-law since the death of your husband – how you left your father and mother and your homeland and came to live with a people you did not know before. May the Lord repay you for what you have done. May you be richly rewarded by the Lord, the God of Israel, under whose wings you have come to take refuge."*

As carers we can be greatly encouraged by the story of Ruth, who was blessed by God because He recognised her selfless devotion to someone who needed her support.

Ruth was very forward and upward looking. I don't think she saw her ministering as just serving Naomi or denying herself anything, but as a life being lived out for God. As the story progresses, we can see how God brought the strands of her life together in order to fulfil His purposes through her. As a result she was richly rewarded by Him. I believe God can also do this for us.

For reflection and action:

≈ *Service for God does not go unseen or unrewarded.*

≈ *"Lord, please help me to make the right choices."*

Knowing
God

"I want to know Christ."

Philippians 3:10

As carers we are very much in need of God's help and strength in our lives, and this can only come through our relationship with Him. Perhaps you feel in need of reassurance in this area, or may even be wondering where to begin.

There was a period in my life when I was very aware of my need of God. During this time I came to know some "real" Christians who had a living faith and talked about God as though He was a friend to them. I knew that they had found what I was searching for, and I became all the more determined in my quest for truth and reality.

I wanted a relationship with God, mainly because I had what I could only describe as a God-shaped blank in my life. I knew that I was not a complete person, and never could be until this problem was sorted out. I tried many roads in my search for God, getting more and more desperate as time went by. One day I shut myself in my room, got down on my knees and cried out to God. I said something like, "Please God help me, I'm desperate to know You, I've got a big aching gap inside that only You can fill, I need You God, please take over my life, and make me Your child."

There were no flashes of lightning or any spectacular happenings which I imagined might accompany an encounter with God, but I knew that He had heard my prayer and met with me. The emptiness had gone, and was replaced by an amazing sense of peace, such as I'd not experienced before. I had an overwhelming assurance that everything was all right between me and God.

Have you ever seen a shop with big notices across the windows, proclaiming, "Under new management"? Well that is exactly how I felt from the moment I'd prayed that prayer. I knew that I now belonged to Jesus and that I had entered into a living relationship with Him. There were changes to follow, and things in my life that needed to be put right, but I knew I had been "born again" as it says in John's Gospel.

Everybody's experience is different, but God gives this new life to all who seek Him in sincerity. Maybe you have met with God in the past, but feel that the relationship has gone a bit stale, or perhaps you are aware of the need to deepen your commitment to Him. Well, there is no time like the present. In 2 Corinthians 6:2 Paul says, *"I tell you, now is the time of God's favour, now is the day of salvation"*. It is always now with God, we never have to wait for any reason, we can always do business with God. So take a few minutes now, speak to God and allow Him to speak to you. Trust Him, and put yourself in His hands, for He is trustworthy.

For reflection and action:

❧ *Meditate on John 14:6 and John 20:31*

❧ *Jesus gives life with a capital L.*

Making the Most of Each Day

"This is the day the Lord has made." Psalm 118:24

Are you bored or depressed? Does it seem to you as though life goes on in humdrum fashion, an ongoing routine with little or no variety in it, as though days, weeks, even months, have been programmed in an unalterable way? As a carer it may be that you see things like this because the rhythm of life appears to be dictated by other people's needs, and you feel as though you are on an invisible treadmill. Be assured, God knows how you feel.

We know from Ecclesiastes 3:2 that there is a time to be born and a time to die, in fact a time for everything on earth. But within this framework of God's plan for our lives is tremendous scope for variety and creativity. Let's stop for a moment and think how creative God is. He is creating and recreating the whole time, He never stops. He created heaven and earth, day and night, you and me, and every expression of nature around us, and nature itself is in a constant state of change and development.

Do you realise that today is a very special day? It is new, there has never been another like it and never will be. God has given us this whole new day spread out before us like a clean slate or a field of untrodden snow, for us to live and enjoy and mark with our own personality. Creativity is finding new ways to express ourselves, to find an outlet for hidden depths of our own inventiveness and imagination, and the more we can let ourselves go in these areas, the less mundane our lives will be.

I want to shake off the idea that my day is to be ruled by the entries in my diary, and allow it to be coloured by the vivacity of my God-given personality. Creativity does not have to imply greatness, like the skills of a master craftsman, but can have small beginnings within our daily lives, and can be discovered in numerous ways, always bringing a sense of achievement, fulfilment and pleasure.

We have a creative God, let us learn from Him, and find new outlets for self-expression in everything we do today. I want to allow my mind to be stretched, and push out the limiting concepts which I have believed for so long about "always doing things the same way", always "writing notes this way". Write a poem instead, I'm sure the milkman won't mind, it will probably lighten his day too!

Creativity brings revitalisation to stagnant areas of the mind, and can be so refreshing and rejuvenating.

I am so glad that this is the day that the Lord has made, let us rejoice and be glad in it.

For reflection and action:

❧ *Remember that today you will be making tomorrow's memories. Would you prefer them in Technicolor or monochrome?*

❧ *Ask God to help you unlock those hidden depths.*

Knowing my Value

"God has arranged the parts in the body, every one of them, just as he wanted them to be."

1 Corinthians 12:18

As believers, we are likened in Scripture to a body, each a different part with a different function, and together we make up the body of Christ, who is the Head.

I wonder how you see yourself in this context, and how much value you would put on your contribution to the whole. Paul tells us in 1 Corinthians 12, that we are all of vital importance, and that we should not in any way belittle our worth. Here are some extracts from this passage of Scripture:

> "Now the body is not made up of one part but of many" (v.14).

> "God has arranged the parts in the body, every one of them, just as he wanted them to be" (v.18).

> "The eye cannot say to the hand, 'I don't need you!' And the head cannot say to the feet, 'I don't need you!' On the contrary, those parts of the body that seem to be weaker are indispensable, and the parts that we think are less honourable we treat with special honour. And the parts that are unpresentable are treated with special modesty, while our presentable parts need no special treatment. But God has combined the members of the body and has given greater honour to the parts that lacked it, so that there should be no division in the body, but that its parts should have equal concern for each other. If one part suffers, every part suffers with it; if one part is honoured, every part rejoices with it" (vv.21–26).

Have you ever thought about how much care and maintenance each part of the body requires? We like to keep our bodies in good condition so we wash them, feed and exercise them. The more we give out to others, the more we need to be revived and refreshed ourselves. So as carers we should realise our need to be also on the receiving end, and allow others to minister to us. We often find it so much easier to recognise other people's needs than our own, but we have a responsibility to look after ourselves as part of Christ's body.

Try asking yourself a few questions, like, do I feel cared for by other Christians? Do I feel supported, or do I feel out on a limb? Do I have needs that I find too difficult to speak about? Even though I may be capable and independent, are there areas where I could do with some help? Then look at who your friends are, and decide if there is someone with whom you can share your feelings and concerns. It would be good and helpful to find someone who is outside your family situation, so that they can bring in a fresh perspective. If no one comes to mind, then ask God to provide someone for you. You need mutual support.

The other thing to look at is how tied and tired you feel, and whether you are getting a regular break from the work-side of your commitment, and see if you need someone to stand in the gap for you. Don't be afraid to ask for help, these things can bring revitalisation to you, a vital part of the body of Christ.

For reflection and action:

❧ *If one part suffers, every part suffers with it; if one part is honoured, every part rejoices with it.*

❧ *"Lord help me to see the significance of my role in your body."*

My
Goal

"Let us fix our eyes on Jesus."

Hebrews 12:2

Carers are as diverse a people as you would find anywhere, a complete cross-section of society, not marked out by wealth, age, sex or colour. Some live-in, some care from a distance, some part-time, some full-time. However, we will find that there are a number of similarities. They are mostly people with caring hearts, many of whom make numerous sacrifices in order to fit in with the needs of others.

They also encounter common difficulties, one of them being the unpredictability of life from day to day, and with it the difficulty of planning ahead. To those of us in such a position it can at times seem as though our lives are being ruled by demands beyond our control, so that we are unable to make our own decisions. But let us realise that however much we make ourselves available to the needs of others, everything we do comes within the wider context of our life in God and His purposes for each of us.

Paul had one goal in life, which he never lost sight of, namely to know God in a deeper way. Even though he led a very busy life, with much travelling and preaching, it all came within the context of his goal. Even when he was imprisoned, he referred to himself as an ambassador in chains. Paul speaks about his one great goal in life in Philippians 3. Beginning at verse 10, he says, *"I want to know Christ and the power of his resurrection and the fellowship of sharing in his sufferings . . . I press on to take hold of that for which Christ took hold of me . . . But one thing I do: Forgetting what is behind and straining towards what is ahead, I press on towards the goal to win the prize for which*

God has called me heavenwards in Christ Jesus." He saw clearly the direction in which he was going and allowed nothing to sidetrack him.

We too can have goals in life. If we have come to a place of personal commitment to Christ, then it is likely that we know where we are heading and what our desires and aims are, and even though our everyday life may be taken up with a hundred and one other things, they need not interfere with the all-encompassing greatness yet simplicity of our major goal. *"Let us run with perseverance the race marked out for us. Let us fix our eyes on Jesus, the author and perfecter of our faith"* (Hebrews 12:1–2).

For reflection and action:

⮞ *Do I need to refocus on what my main aim is in life?*

⮞ *Lord help me to fulfil my calling in You.*

Day 16

Renewal

"Those who hope in the Lord will renew their strength."
Isaiah 40:31

The whole of our Christian life is built on our *hope* in God, this is why I am glad that the word hope in the Bible has a far more positive meaning than the way we use it today. Today it is an uncertain word, often with a note of caution and a big IF. But in the Bible we have a sure and certain hope, based on God's covenant, in which He has committed Himself to us, through the death of Jesus for all time, a sacrifice to take away sins, which cannot be changed (Hebrews 6:17,18).

This is the foundation of our hope in God, from whom we can receive strength and renewal. In Isaiah 40:28–31 we have some wonderful promises for those who hope in the Lord.

"Do you not know? Have you not heard? The Lord is the everlasting God, the Creator of the ends of the earth. He will not grow tired or weary, and his understanding no-one can fathom. He gives strength to the weary and increases the power of the weak. Even youths grow tired and weary, and young men stumble and fall; but those who hope in the Lord will renew their strength. They will soar on wings like eagles; they will run and not grow weary, they will walk and not be faint."

As a carer I'm sure you know what it is to become tired and weary, but here we are told that we can rise above everyday circumstances in God's strength, and we can know His supernatural power at work in our lives, if our hope is in Him. How we all need this renewing strength. Let us learn to receive from God in new ways, let us adjust our thinking, so that when we are feeling weak, we see this as the very opportunity to receive from God in order to keep going, and have our spirit lifted.

I remember a few years ago, when on holiday in France, we saw an eagle soaring. It went higher and higher as we watched it through binoculars, until it became a tiny speck, and eventually vanished from sight. The way it achieved this was effortless, because it knew how to find the source of power it needed to be carried up. This eagle had found thermals of warm air, and all it had to do was to spread its wings and leave the rest to the currents.

This is a beautiful picture of how we can rest in God and find new strength. When we open up ourselves to His renewing love, we can know the elevating power of his Spirit filling us. When we allow God to take over the control of our lives in this way, we can experience renewal in every part of our life.

This doesn't lessen the problems around us, nor reduce the everyday demands, but we can be free from the downward drag, and free to overcome the feeling of weight which responsibility often imposes on us.

For reflection and action:

🍃 *Allow yourself to be supernaturally supported and see things from a different perspective.*

🍃 *Ask God to take you higher.*

Strength
to Go On

"I have had enough, Lord."

1 Kings 19:4

Today we are looking at my favourite Old Testament story. It is too long to print, so you can read it for yourself from 1 Kings 18–19:9.

We read how Elijah, the great man of God, staged a contest on Mount Carmel to prove the power and reality of God to the powers of darkness. He challenged the evil king Ahab and the prophets of Baal to call down fire from their gods, and Elijah would also call on his God to send fire. We read how the day-long contest ended with Elijah's prayer being answered and God sending fire from heaven. Not only were the prophets of Baal utterly defeated, they were also destroyed.

It was an exhausting day, but God had not yet finished. Elijah had prophesied that rain would come. He went back up the mountain, on his knees sought the fulfilment of his expectation, and God sent the long awaited rain. Then Elijah knew that his task for the day was complete.

Now he ran like he'd never run before. He ran for two reasons to escape the heavy rainstorm and was because he was so afraid of Jezebel, Ahab's wife, who made angry threats, and vowed to kill Elijah because she was a Baal worshipper. It says in Chapter 19:3, *"Elijah was afraid, and ran for his life."* When he eventually stopped, he was completely exhausted, depressed, demoralised and just wanted to die.

It's unlikely that any of us have been through what Elijah went through, and are never likely to. But it is not difficult to identify with the feelings that he experienced at the end of the day, when he'd given everything he'd got and was almost in a state of collapse. He had nothing left to give, and could not imagine that he ever would have. He lay down to sleep, hoping he wouldn't wake up again. I hope our experience doesn't reach that extreme, but I know it is possible.

I know that as carers, many of us have experienced times like that, when we've dreaded facing another day and wondered how we could go on.

We might have thought that the answer for Elijah would be a good night's sleep, then up for a quiet time praying for his needs to be met, but God had other plans.

God had provided for Elijah in the past in various ways; in Chapter 17 God sent ravens to feed Elijah, then further on, he was provided for by a widow woman. But now that Elijah was really at rock bottom, God sent an angel to minister to him (19:5–7). What a wonderful expression of God's love and provision. God not only met Elijah at his point of desperate need, but He encouraged and strengthened him to get up and go on again.

Don't despair if you feel as though you are almost at rock bottom, God has not given up on you. His blessing and encouragement is never dependent on how we feel. He sees and knows our needs even before we ask, so let us trust Him to see us through each day. He has promised that He will not leave us or forsake us.

For reflection and action:

&❧ *Elijah was a man after God's own heart, and God was not going to let him give up.*

&❧ *Find someone to share your needs with before you reach a state of exhaustion.*

Day 18

Counting
Your
Blessings

"Let us come before him with thanksgiving." Psalm 95:2

In much of Paul's teaching in the New Testament, he exhorts us to thankfulness. In Ephesians 5:19 he says, *"Sing and make music in your heart to the Lord, always giving thanks to God the Father for everything, in the name of our Lord Jesus Christ".*

This is something which is sadly lacking in many of us, and in society in general. We are taught from a very early age to say "Thank you", because it is the polite thing to do, but often we learn it parrot-fashion, without really stopping to think about true gratitude of heart. And even when we really do appreciate something, we don't always express it, so it stays uncommunicated. I don't know why we are such negative beings, but many of us concentrate on the difficulties and what we are missing out on in life, and keep insisting that the other person's grass is greener than our own.

Paul's gratitude always came out of an overflowing heart for all that God has done in Christ, and a realisation of God's love for him. Thus he constantly encouraged believers to continue in the faith, and grasp more of God's plan of salvation. In Colossians 2:6-7 he says, *"So then, just as you received Christ Jesus as Lord, continue to live in him ... strengthened in the faith as you were taught, and overflowing with thankfulness."*

I believe that if we understood half of what is in God's heart for us, we would continually be prostrating ourselves before Him in adoration and worship.

When we lead busy lives, and spend a lot of our time caring for others, we find we have little time for ourselves, and it may be that we don't stop and count our blessings as often as we could. Somehow it takes a conscious effort. But as soon as we start to do this, we can be lifted up on to a higher plane, one where we can sing and praise and find that our spirits start to soar. This has a wonderful side effect, because a joyful, grateful attitude can be infectious and help raise the spirits of others too.

I have fond memories of my grandfather, who was one of the most grateful people I have ever known. He often told me, almost with tears, how blessed and privileged he'd been all through his life. He did not have a lot of this world's riches, but he had a simple yet firm faith in God, and he recognised that God had blessed him in numerous ways.

One day, when he was 88, he didn't feel very well and the doctor was called. The doctor could not find any specific problem, but said that he was slowing down and just needed to take life quietly. My grandfather had always been a great cricketing enthusiast and said to the doctor, "Well I've had a great innings!" Later that day my grandfather had a stroke from which he never regained consciousness. He was grateful to the end.

The psalmist knew how to praise God with a thankful heart. In Psalm 34:1 he says, *"I will extol the Lord at all times; his praise will always be on my lips ..."*

For reflection and action:

❧ *Lord I am continually grateful for ...*

❧ *Are there things in your life for which you have never thanked God? You could start today!*

Courage

"Be strong ... the Lord your God
will be with you." Joshua 1:9

The children of Israel had spent forty years wandering in the wilderness, now all that was about to change. They had arrived at the place where they would enter the Promised Land. This was a new beginning in every sense. They had never been here before, and God was leading them into new territory. They literally had to follow Him one step at a time. God had told them to be strong and courageous, to not be terrified or discouraged, for He would be with them wherever they went. They had to listen, obey and follow. The key to this new venture was, "The Lord your God will be with you".

I find these principles very encouraging for our everyday life. As carers we often face new situations with which we have had no experience, or going into places where we've not been before. Much of what we experience develops slowly, so we hardly notice the changes. But at other times it seems our lives are taken over by events around us, which can loom large and daunting. But the principles are the same.

If we are willing to stay close to God, and ready to listen to Him and follow, then He will lead us and guide us, and we have nothing to fear about stepping out into the unknown.

Another parallel in this passage with which we can identify is the way that Joshua had to change roles. This is something which often happens in caring for people, maybe not in the same way as for Joshua, but we are constantly reminded of our need for change and flexibility.

Following the death of Moses, Joshua was told by God to lead the children of Israel into the Promised

Land. This could have been very difficult for Joshua because in Deuteronomy 34:12 we read, *"No one has ever shown the mighty power or performed the awesome deeds that Moses did in the sight of all Israel."* Poor Joshua had to follow that!

But even this potential difficulty had been foreseen. In Deuteronomy 34:9 we read *"Joshua ... was filled with the spirit of wisdom because Moses had laid his hands on him. So the Israelites listened to him."* Joshua was neither at a loss, nor at a disadvantage, because he was following God and Moses had prayed for him.

So we can see from this the importance of having an ongoing, living relationship with God, knowing that we are in the place where He wants us to be, and going in the right direction; and having someone to pray for us, so that we have the ability to fulfil the task He has called us to. This may be an occasion for someone within the church to lay hands on us and pray, or it may be a friend who is willing to pray regularly for us, but we need to be supported by prayer. Now let us take to heart God's words to Joshua, *"Be strong and courageous ... for the Lord your God will be with you wherever you go."*

For reflection and action:

❦ *Help me Lord to keep in step with you, as we go forward together.*

❦ *Recognise that receiving support from friends, is not a weakness but a strength.*

God's
Workmanship

"I praise you because I am fearfully and wonderfully made."

Psalm 139:14

God not only created me and formed me in my mother's womb, but since the time I became His child, He has been continually at work in my life, moulding and shaping me, as I am being transformed into His likeness, with ever increasing glory. God's purpose for my life is that I should become like Him. God is the master craftsman, developing me like the potter kneads and fashions the clay, and purifying me as a refiner of gold or silver. This is something which God does in my life in proportion to my willingness. It all depends on how much I want to change and grow.

Have you ever seen a potter at work as he takes a lump of raw clay, and with all his dexterity and expertise, he forms it into something beautiful and unique. I learnt pottery at school, and I know that it takes a great deal of patience, experience and commitment to produce anything of value. But God perseveres with us. The prophet Isaiah says, *"O Lord, you are our Father. We are the clay, you are the potter; we are all the work of your hand"* (Isaiah 64:8). God is committed to working in every department of my life where He has access.

The Bible also likens God's dealings with us to that of a gold or silver refiner. This craft required a lot of care as the refiner sat beside a pan of molten metal and skimmed off the dross which rose to the surface. This process took much time and attention, and would only be complete when the refiner could see his face reflected in the precious metal.

It would be easy for us to think that growth in our lives happens through the good things with which we are blessed, and the high spots which leave us with lasting memories. This may be true, but it is even more true to say that God uses the difficult times and hardships to strengthen our character and bring us further on our journey along the road to maturity. Let us take heart, knowing that whatever we face in our daily lives, God can use as an opportunity for us to prove Him in new ways. Often as a carer life can seem to be negative, with a sense of isolation, helplessness and uncertainty, and numerous other hurdles to overcome, but these obstacles can all be faced and dealt with in God's development of me as a person. Our circumstances may not alter, but God can reshape our thinking, so that we can see more from His perspective the new creation that He is working on, as He transforms our life.

Paul probably suffered more in his Christian life than we shall ever experience, including imprisonment, stoning, flogging, shipwreck and going without food and sleep, yet he could say *"... but we also rejoice in our sufferings, because we know that suffering produces perseverance; perseverance, character; and character, hope"* (Romans 5:3–4).

For reflection and action:

❧ *My life in God is a living process towards maturity.*

❧ *Help me Lord to see any difficult circumstances as your opportunities.*

Victory

"Be strong in the Lord and in
his mighty power."
Ephesians 6:10

Caring can be hard work, enjoyable yes, but also exhausting. We can so easily get bogged down with all the regular routine we have to perform each day, plus the unexpected, and before we know it we are feeling low and vulnerable to the attacks of Satan. We are constantly reminded in the New Testament, that our greatest enemy is not in the problems surrounding us, but the unseen enemy of our souls, who is constantly seeking to undermine us and destroy our peace of mind.

So life in one sense is a battle. If God has His place as Lord in our life then Satan has a vested interest in breaking down that stronghold. But don't give up. Let us remember we are on the winning side, God has already defeated Satan on the cross, and has provided all the resources for us to keep him at bay in our lives. *"Be prepared. You're up against far more than you can handle on your own. Take all the help you can get, use every weapon God has issued, so that when it's all over but the shouting you'll still be on your feet. Truth righteousness, peace, faith and salvation are more than words. Learn how to apply them.*

You'll need them throughout your life. God's Word is an indispensable weapon. In the same way, prayer is essential in this ongoing warfare. Pray hard and long." These words are from Ephesians 6 in *The Message.*

Prayer is the hardest thing of all, maybe because it requires the greatest measure of discipline, I don't know, but I do know that the majority of Christians struggle in this area. Yet this is the greatest gift available to us, all day and every day, the opportunity of communication with God, the connection from earth to heaven. Without communication, we are either living in unreality or history, but with prayer at our disposal we can know the living ongoing reality of walking with God. There are different kinds of prayer, and varying depths of prayer. We can talk to God anywhere and anytime, but to allow ourselves to hear and receive from God involves giving our time, and shutting out everything else. This can be costly, but can also reap great rewards. This is where the battles are won and the victories claimed. Let us make this our starting point.

"The earnest, heartfelt, continued prayer of a righteous man makes tremendous power available – dynamic in its working" (James 5:16, Amplified Bible).

For reflection and action:

❧ *Prayer changes things.*

❧ *The victory is ours for the claiming.*

Day 22

Shared
Burdens

"Cast your cares on the Lord."

Psalm 55:22

Do you ever feel overburdened? Most people do at some time or other. It is not unusual, but it is important how we handle the situation. As a carer we may find ourselves carrying extra responsibilities which bring their own pressures to bear on us. We read a lot in the Scriptures about burdens, and there are a number of different meanings to the word.

The dictionary suggests words like, obligation, oppressive duty, expense or emotion, however the implication of Scripture is that a burden is basically something to be borne. If we bear that burden in relationship with Jesus, it is light, but when we carry it alone the heavier and more depressing it becomes.

In the teachings of Jesus we read on several occasions of His comparison to the burden carried by oxen ploughing the fields, and of the difference between using the rough mass-produced wooden yoke, and the craftsman-designed one that was purpose-made, so that it fitted perfectly without rubbing and chafing the animal. He tells us that if we are yoked together in harmony with Him, we will find that His yoke is the perfectly fitting variety, and working in unison with Him we will find that our task or burden is light. He says in Matthew 11:28–30, *"Come to me, all you who are weary and burdened, and I will give you rest. Take my yoke upon you and learn from me, for I am gentle and humble in heart, and you will find rest for your souls. For my yoke is easy and my burden is light."*

Another reference to burdens relates to the burden bearer. This was a common sight in Bible times, and still is in some countries today. Strong men who earned their living by carrying heavy goods could be seen slowly plodding along the road under huge loads of luggage, or furniture, then when they needed to rest they would stop and another man would come alongside and either put his shoulder under the burden and take the weight for five or ten minutes, or else the weight would be transferred by rolling the burden over from one man's back to the other. Straightaway we can see the significance of this in Scripture. In Psalm 55:22 from the Amplified Version we read: *"Cast your burden on the Lord releasing the weight of it, and He will sustain you. He will never allow the righteous to be moved, made to slip, fail or fall."*

So our problem is not having burdens, but rather how we handle them.

If you feel burdened today, stop for a moment in the presence of God, and find out what the burden is all about. Do you need the help of Jesus so that as you work together in partnership you can experience the joy of a shared lightweight burden? Or are you carrying a burden that you don't need to carry at all? If so, ask Jesus to come alongside so that you can make a transfer. I am quoting again from the Amplified Version from 1 Peter 5:7, *"Casting the whole of your care, all your anxieties, all your worries, all your concerns, once and for all, on Him, for He cares for you affectionately, and cares about you watchfully."*

For reflection and action:

❧ *Carrying a burden may be a necessity, carrying it alone is optional.*

❧ *Try and express your feelings to God in prayer.*

Daily
Trust

"… you do not know what a day
may bring forth."

Proverbs 27:1

As carers, I believe that we are more than ever aware of the uncertainty of each day, and our constant need to be ready for anything. So often situations arise that we are unprepared for, and we find ourselves dependent on God alone as we offer up a quick, and sometimes desperate prayer, to know how to cope with the unexpected. It is at times like this that our faith and trust is most tested. In Proverbs 3:5–6 we read: *"Trust in the Lord with all your heart and lean not on your own understanding; in all your ways acknowledge him, and he will make your paths straight."*

God has given us a whole range of natural abilities to use in our everyday lives, and as we live in relationship with Him He can be glorified through them. How amazing it is that we can take on responsibilities, plan ahead and use our understanding to work things out practically – all the time using gifts which God has given to us.

However, there are times when we need to allow all this to be transcended by our dependence on God and trust Him totally, not seeing the end from the beginning or even the next step to take, but just to allow Him to take the reins of our life and lead us on. He has promised to illuminate the path ahead.

Trust cannot be planned in advance. We can decide to trust God for the future, but real trusting only happens while it is in operation, and is most crucial in an unknown situation.

The need to be able to trust came home very forcibly to me in a recent experience I had while on holiday in Switzerland. I was offered the chance to parachute off a mountain. I am normally a very cautious person, but the idea appealed to me so strongly that I was faced with a dilemma – Shall I? Shan't I? I must hasten to add that we are talking about a two-man parachute with an experienced parachutist. So it all basically came down to my trust in this man. I decided to go for it. We shook hands and I agreed to follow any instructions I was given. He said to me, "It's easy – I shall say one, two, three, go, and you start running, don't slow down, don't stop when you get to the edge, just keep your feet going in running steps so that you will eventually find yourself running in the air." We were harnessed together with the parachute. The trust came into operation when he said "GO." It seemed I only ran four or five paces and my feet were off the ground. It was one of the most wonderful experiences I have ever had – which I would have missed if I had not been able to trust my guide. How much more trustworthy is our God. Psalm 118:8 says, *"It is better to take refuge in the Lord than to trust in man."*

Job probably went through the darkest, most despairing, heart-rending times that any human being could face, but he had a very sure foundation. He declared that he wouldn't stop trusting God, even if it cost him his life (Job 13:15).

For reflection and action:

❧*Trust is most crucial in the unknown, yet nothing is unknown to God.*

❧*We don't know what the future holds, but we know the One who holds the future.*

Look
Up

"Let us fix our eyes on Jesus, the author and perfecter of our faith." Hebrews 12:2

The author is the only one who knows how the story will end! To know that Jesus started the whole scenario of my life and will bring it to completion is a very secure place to be in. Everything we have committed to Him comes under His lordship and within His control. We read in Ecclesiastes that there is a time to be born and a time to die, in fact a time for everything under heaven, and it has all been planned by God. We are exhorted to keep our eyes on Him, so we don't miss anything we want to know, what He's saying and where He's leading us. Keeping eye contact is one of the more intimate ways of communication and of really getting to know and understand another person. It is also an attitude of worship and adoration.

When I was taken to church as a child, it always puzzled me why people who were praying to God up there in heaven had their heads down as though they were looking at the floor. Of course, I now realise that they had their heads bowed in reverence, but with the same childlike simplicity we can look up into the face of our heavenly Father and see Him as our God, the Creator and finisher of our faith. Whether we have our eyes open or closed doesn't matter, it is the attitude of looking up that symbolises keeping our eyes fixed on heavenly things.

Being a carer can bring its own difficulties, I know there are days for some of us when we don't feel like looking up. All around is gloom and doom, and there seems to be an impenetrable cloud between us and God.

The psalmist often had black days like this where

God seemed to be nowhere around, but many times, when he looked up and reached out to God, he would break into spontaneous praise. In Psalm 34, David had been through a dark and difficult time, fearing for his life, but he was able to reach out and find God who was the beginning and end for him – the all-embracing God. He said, *"I sought the Lord, and he answered me; he delivered me from all my fears. Those who look to him are radiant; their faces are never covered with shame"* (vv. 4–6).

Have you ever stopped to think that however cold or grey the day may be, the sun is always shining. You only have to go up in an aeroplane for the proof of this; as soon as you get above the clouds there it is. In a similar way God is always God. He is the same yesterday, today and forever. He never changes, never leaves us and never stops loving us.

Paul could say in Philippians 1:6, *"... he who began a good work in you will carry it on to completion."* So keep looking up to Jesus.

For reflection and action:

❧ *However we feel, we can choose whether we look up to Jesus, or down to the things around us.*

❧ *Two men looked out from behind the same bars, one saw mud, the other saw stars.*

Lifeline

" ... apart from me you can do nothing." John 15:5.

J esus has given us a lovely illustration of how we can be one with Him. He says in John 15:1,5 *"I am the true vine and my Father is the gardener . . . you are the branches. If a man remains in me and I in Him, he will bear much fruit; apart from me you can do nothing."*

This is particularly relevant for those who feel isolated, and I know that this can be a problem for many who are carers, who find themselves very limited in their involvement with people and activities outside the home.

In this passage we can see that however isolated we may feel, we need never be solitary. As Christians we are part of a healthy, fruitful vine. We are a vital, useful part of a life-giving organism. Can you imagine a vine, which is constantly and lovingly tended by a skilled gardener? One planted and trained in a special way to receive the maximum benefits of warmth and daylight, probably fed with extra nutrition and regularly watered, so as to produce the finest fruit. One that would be systematically pruned and checked daily for any problems which might arise.

Let us try to imagine the care and love of God which is implied here. We can be in such a secure and all-sufficient place that all our life's requirements can be drawn from Jesus, with His life flowing through us. No wonder that He says, *"without me you can do nothing."* We are totally dependent on Him for everything, yet we can trust Him to live out His life through us.

We may be thinking to ourselves, but how can I bear fruit? I'm at home most of the day, or dashing from one place to another. The fruit of the Christian life is symbolised in character development in which God is continually at work in our lives, often when we are least aware of the fact.

These fruits of His Spirit will grow and develop as we remain in Him, and constantly draw our needs and sustenance from His life-giving source. We know that the type and quality of the fruit which is produced will depend on our being totally united with Him. Remember that even though the fruit is seen on the branches, it is the parent plant which gives life.

For reflection and action:

❧ *Ponder on the security of feeling one with Christ.*

❧ *Remember God is constantly at work in our lives.*

Peace
in the
Storm

"Then the wind died down and it
was completely calm."

Mark 4:39

Today let us read about the storm described in Mark 4:35–39.

"That day when evening came, he said to his disciples, 'Let us go over to the other side'. Leaving the crowd behind, they took him along, just as he was, in the boat. There were also other boats with him. A furious squall came up, and the waves broke over the boat, so that it was nearly swamped. Jesus was in the stern, sleeping on a cushion. The disciples woke him and said to him, 'Teacher, don't you care if we drown?' He got up, rebuked the wind and said to the waves, 'Quiet! Be still!' Then the wind died down and it was completely calm."

It must have been a terrifying experience for the disciples to have been in such a storm. I can imagine that all their natural reactions of fear were aroused to such a pitch that they were nearly hysterical by the time they woke Jesus. How could He just sleep on, disregarding their plight? How could any normal person just switch off in such a time of crisis?

In our day-to-day routine as carers, we may sometimes share these feelings of frustration when we hit a crisis and it seems as though nobody is there to understand, or help us find a way to deal with it. We might even know the sense of fear and anger which the disciples experienced as they were overwhelmed by their inadequacy to do anything. How we need to know God's peace at times like this. In this passage of Scripture, Jesus demonstrates two kinds of peace, inner peace and outward peace. Both are beyond natural human experience, they are God's supernatural gifts.

Imagine the turmoil that was going on, with the boat being buffeted and the shouting of frightened men, and here was Jesus sound asleep and at peace through it all. Then when Jesus had been woken up, there was one calm, peaceful man in the boat and a number of frightened, angry ones. It was the one with the inner calm who took the situation in hand and dealt with the cause of all the problems. He spoke with the authority of God and brought outward peace to reign where there had been chaos and turbulence.

Our faith and trust in God needs to extend beyond our natural experience for us to know His supernatural power at work in us.

How can we know inner peace? It is a gift of God which we can ask for in simple faith. In John 14:27, when Jesus was about to leave His disciples here on earth, He said to them (and to those who would follow after them), *"Peace I leave with you; my peace I give you. I do not give to you as the world gives."* In Philippians 4:7 Paul says: *"... the peace of God, which transcends all understanding, will guard your hearts and your minds in Christ Jesus."* So ask God to give you this inner peace which defies human understanding and comes from the indwelling of his Holy Spirit. This inner peace will then give you the strength and confidence to deal with the storms of life.

For reflection and action:

✤ *Do you believe that if Jesus said, "Let us go over to the other side", He would let you sink halfway?*

✤ *Ask Jesus for His promise of peace to become your experience.*

Follow
my Leader

"I will instruct you and teach you
in the way you should go."
Psalm 32:8

Have you ever been on one of those conducted tours where a guide is in control who shares some information, then moves on and says, "Follow me", and in some cases shines a torch on the path ahead to show the way?

This illustrates something of how God guides us through life's journey. Not only has He promised to do so, but He uses various means to achieve His purpose and lead us safely through to our destination.

One of the key features of His guidance is His inspired Word, the Bible, which we could not be without. It is our Maker's manual and comprehensive guidebook to life.

In Psalm 119:105 we read, *"Your word is a lamp to my feet and a light for my path."*

God's Word is such an intrinsic part of the life of a believer that we become impoverished if we neglect to read it. So by reading God's Word, and allowing it to become part of us, we can move forward with God. And conversely, if we don't give it the value and importance it deserves, we are denying ourselves great opportunities for expansion and growth. Through God's Word I can become a wealthier and more enlightened person, with this light of life pointing me in the right direction.

In our day to day situations as carers, we can find limitless resources at our disposal through God's Word. In times of isolation, when we feel as though we are travelling alone, remember Jesus has said that He will never leave us nor forsake us.

Once when I was meditating on the amazing fact that I could know God's guidance, I wrote this poem:

"Stay close to me," my guide said, as through the dark he led,

His torch shone very brightly on the pathway just ahead.

When I stayed within earshot, his words were clear to me,

He pointed out the hazards, and the things I couldn't see.

When I stayed close beside him, I felt secure and calm,

His steady arm upheld me, and kept me safe from harm.

We crossed some deep dark waters I could not cross alone,

He knew the way, he'd been before, to me it was unknown.

He showed me things that in his light, were beautiful to see,

The rainbow, and the sunset, the ever-pounding sea,

The perfume of a cowslip, the humming of a bee,

The softness of a new-born lamb, the grandeur of a tree.

The air was warm and balmy, the pathway smoother here,

The pace of life slowed down, while I had time to stop and stare,

To taste, to smell, to listen, to feel, to think, to see.

It pleased him that I lingered, then he whispered, "Follow me."

For reflection and action:

❧ *God always takes the initiative, and it's His desire to guide us.*

❧ *Let us always remember to stay close to Him.*

Why?

"Now I know in part; then I shall know fully." 1 Corinthians 13:12

Have you ever asked the question why? Why me? Why this? This is a particularly pertinent question for carers, because we so often find ourselves in a situation where there seems to be no solution, no reason and no understanding as to why or how our circumstances have come about in a certain way.

At this moment I am thinking especially of those caring for someone since the day they were born, which could be days, months or even decades – a way of life they would never have visualised, a situation that they imagined could only ever happen to others.

Our loved one, our gift from God, has been found to be needing special care and attention because of their physical condition, and it is likely that we see them as extra special because they are different, and they have individual needs which only we can appreciate. To us they have a unique value, like a secret between the two of us and God, which may only be shared with a few close members of our family. Nevertheless the questions remain unanswered.

The medical profession may be able to tell us which category our loved one comes under, and give us sympathetic advice about their requirements, but may not be able to tell us why they were born like this. Onlookers may have even more problems with their unanswered questions, and make patronising comments like, "Oh, poor thing", or "However do you manage?", which could be coming out of a sense of curiosity or idle reflection, rather than sincere concern or a desire to help.

In the situation we are in we can't pretend to have

the answers. For many of us there will be dark moments and sleepless nights when we may find ourselves groaning from deep within, or crying out to God, not always looking for answers, but saying Why God? Why did it happen? How much longer? What of the future? Many of these questions have no answer this side of heaven. But I know from experience that God comforts the troubled soul, and as we reach out to Him we can know His love and peace in ever increasing measure. I also know that He brings tremendous fulfilment through caring for someone we love, even though it may only be a one-sided relationship.

Our understanding in this life is rather like looking in the sort of mirrors that were used in Bible times, very poor forerunners of our modern mirrors, where the image was clouded, distorted and very limited. But when we meet Jesus in glory then everything will be revealed clearly. *"Now we see but a poor reflection as in a mirror; then we shall see face to face. Now I know in part; then I shall know fully, even as I am fully known"* (1 Corinthians 13:12).

For reflection and action:

❧ *Don't let what you don't know spoil what you do know.*

❧ *Learn to trust God with the things you don't understand.*

Trust
for
Tomorrow?

"Do not worry about tomorrow ..." Matthew 6:34

Do you worry about tomorrow? Do you inwardly struggle to work out whether there will be enough money for food, clothes and mortgage? And what about resources and help needed in the home?

Maybe you could really do with a holiday, but feel tied to the house because as a carer your number one priority is the person that you are caring for, and planning ahead can be difficult and cause a lot of anxiety.

Jesus teaches us in simple terms to trust Him one day at a time, and He will provide on that basis. We may sometimes feel as though we have suddenly run into a crisis, but God is never taken by surprise, He knows our needs better than we know ourselves, God's provision is, PRO (before) VISION (seeing), and it is very reassuring to know that He sees our needs in advance.

In Luke 12, starting at verse 22, Jesus says, *"Do not worry about your life, what you will eat; or about your body, what you will wear. Life is more than food, and the body more than clothes ... Consider how the lilies grow. They do not labour or spin. Yet I tell you, not even Solomon in all his splendour was dressed like one of these. If that is how God clothes the grass of the field, which is here today, and tomorrow is thrown into the fire, how much more will he clothe you ... ."*

What an amazing comparison! Here is Solomon, successful, powerful, the wealthiest and most grandly-dressed man in the world, and Jesus is saying that his splendour is nothing compared to that of the wild flowers in the field around him, that nobody by their efforts can match up to what God has already created.

Just look at the beauty of the wild flowers, they are magnificent beyond the handiwork of any human being, and if God lavishes all that extravagance and care on flowers, then just think for a moment how much more valuable we are to Him than flowers. Let us recognise the simple fact that we are God's creation and have been individually designed to glorify Him with our lives. Let us come to Him just as we are, with childlike trust, and rely on Him as our Father and Creator, our Lord and provider.

"As a father has compassion on his children, so the Lord has compassion on those who fear him; for he knows how we are formed, he remembers that we are dust . . . but from everlasting to everlasting the Lord's love is with those who fear him"(Psalm 103:13–14,17).

Let us take this opportunity to open up ourselves to new areas of trust, and experience a greater dependency on God. By this we can know a greater measure of His faithfulness and provision for our needs. Jesus says, in Luke 12, that if the prime motive of my heart is to seek God's kingdom, then He will provide for my daily needs.

For reflection and action:

❧ *If you feel fearful, don't be afraid to ask someone to pray with you.*

❧ *When God does something in your life, use it as a stepping stone of faith to greater things.*

What of the **Future?**

"He will wipe every tear from their eyes." Revelation 21:4

Do you ever worry about the future? As a carer you may be in the position of responsibility for a loved one who has no hope of ever improving physically or mentally, in fact, your whole life is clouded by the hopelessness of the situation. Does it seem to you as though they are on a downward slope which you are powerless to prevent, and all you know is that the future is very uncertain? In fact it is as though the end is almost in sight. You may even find yourself trying to prepare for the inevitable, by grieving in advance for a person who has not yet died, or trying desperately to store up good memories that you know you'll need. These things may be helpful to ease the pain, but will do little to prevent the sense of loss.

You may believe in the glorious truths of God's Word, knowing that your loved one will be going to a far better place where they will be free from pain and sorrow and rejoicing in God's presence, but you also know that you will be the loser, with a big gap in your life and nothing but memories.

I am writing all this because I want to share my own experience with you. I lost someone very dear to me a long time ago, and in a situation like this we usually clutch to anything we can find to remind us of them. All I had were memories which I had shut away inside me for a number of years. At times it was emotionally draining for me to keep hold of them so tightly, but I didn't know what else to do, I was afraid of losing them, until one day some friends prayed for me. I had an amazing experience of release and afterwards I wrote the following:

A handful of memories

When my loved one died I was left with memories,
Only memories – nothing but memories.
Happy memories of a shared life,
Sad memories of a separating death –
but memories – a handful of memories.
I held them tight – it was all I had.
I couldn't let go – I couldn't see beyond them.
Oh yes, I believed in God and heaven and eternal life,
I had hope for my loved one, eternal hope,
But where could I store my handful of memories?
One day God said, "Hold out your hands to Me,
release all that is dear – trust Me".
It was only as I released my grip,
that my eyes began to open.
I could see what God was showing me,
I could see my loved one free, beyond the confines of
my anxious grasp, free as a bird,
a lovely white dove, free from the pull of gravity,
free from the troubles of life, free to be perfectly free,
and as I let go – I was free too.

For reflection and action:

✤ *The more precious someone is, the more you can trust them to God.*

✤ *Anything given to God is not lost.*